LIVING
ADVENT

A DAILY COMPANION TO THE LECTIONARY
(CYCLE C)

JULIA DUGGER

LIGUORI
PUBLICATIONS

One Liguori Drive
Liguori, MO 63057-9999
(314) 464-2500

Imprimi Potest:
James Shea, C.SS.R.
Provincial, St. Louis Province
The Redemptorists

Imprimatur:
+ Edward J. O'Donnell, D.D.
Auxiliary Bishop, Archdiocese of St. Louis

ISBN 0-89243-698-0
Library of Congress Catalog Card Number: 94-76238

Scripture texts used in the *Lectionary for Mass* are taken from the *New American Bible*, Copyright © 1986 and 1991 by the Confraternity of Christian Doctrine, 3211 Fourth Street, N.E., Washington, DC 20017-1194, and are used with permission. All rights reserved.

Excerpts from the English translation of *The Roman Missal,* copyright © 1973, International Committee on English in the Liturgy, Inc. (ICEL), are used with permission. All rights reserved.

Cover design by Chris Sharp

CONTENTS

INTRODUCTION

The Character of the Season of Advent

What is Advent? The word *advent* comes from the Latin *adventus*, meaning coming or arrival. In the Church's liturgical calendar, Advent is the season of hope in which we prepare to celebrate the commemoration of the first coming of Jesus Christ and look forward to his Second Coming.

The first coming, the birth of the baby Jesus at Bethlehem, is familiar to all of us. In this historical moment, we see the melding of history with eternity as God becomes human. However, Advent also heralds the Second Coming of Christ, the Parousia. In the New Testament, Parousia, a Greek word meaning presence or arrival, indicates the coming of Jesus at the end of time, the fulfillment of the mystery initiated in the first coming at Bethlehem. It is an arrival not to be feared but desired, as the Lord will come in glory as king, vindicating the just in the Last Judgment. Our faith and hope are oriented to this fulfillment of the salvation of the world.

While these two perspectives constitute the Church's official understanding of the season, Advent suggests yet a third coming, one by which the season becomes more than just a time of year, and the liturgy more than mere ceremony: it is the coming of Christ within us. During Advent, the Incarnation should become a personal experience of Christ growing within us through the power of the Holy Spirit. It is a time of new life and of new living, a season of personal hope and potential, of blest and fresh spiritual beginnings. In fact *adventus, advent's* root word, is also the root word for adventure.

The Readings of the Advent Liturgy

Even as the season of Advent has its own particular character, the lectionary readings of the Advent liturgy are selected and arranged to disclose and develop this character by way of certain themes. Each of these themes—the Second Coming of Christ, the figure of John the Baptist, and the events leading up to the birth of Jesus—are essential not only to the unfolding of the liturgical season, but to the life of the Church and its members as well.

The readings of the first week of Advent announce the Lord's coming at the end of time and the establishment of his kingdom. As Christians, we acknowledge that Jesus has already come in history, that he rules in our time, and that he is with us, both in the Church and in the hearts of believers. However, we await and anticipate and "live in joyful hope" of yet another advent, the Second Coming of Jesus, when the mystery of salvation will be fully realized and all things will be one in God, through Christ and in the Holy Spirit. What we now perceive and understand of God "dimly as in a mirror" we will come to see in all its fullness of glory, unity, goodness, truth, beauty, and justice. Jesus, at this time, will advent into his kingdom and rule as both God and man. During this first week of Advent, then, the readings drawn from Hebrew Scripture are rich with prophecies of the Messiah and his kingdom, while the epistle readings exhort us to vigilance and right living, that we might ready ourselves to rejoice in the mystery of the Incarnation and look hopefully toward the full revelation of the mystery of salvation.

The readings of the second and third weeks of Advent concentrate on the figure of John the Baptist, particularly as he bears witness to Jesus as the Christ, the anointed one of God. John, like the Old Testament prophets whose voice and manner he echoes, is called forth to speak in God's stead, and what John continually proclaims is "Jesus!" John shows us the witness that we, too, are called to give, to become prophets crying out "Jesus!" to all the world, testifying to the Word made flesh in all that we say and do.

The readings of the Fourth Sunday of Advent and the late Advent weekdays treat of the events that led directly to the birth of Jesus. These familiar narratives constitute, for us who are members of God's family, our family stories, our spiritual family tree. In recalling these events, we are reminded yet again that the God around whom this family is gathered is a God who has acted concretely in history. We are reminded, too, that God has not merely intervened in human affairs, but rather, in the Christ event, has chosen to share fully in our humanity.

Spiritually, we Christians all begin with Jesus and the indelible mark of the divine that he left on our humanity in his Incarnation. Thus, we celebrate the manner of Jesus' birth, his origins and descent. Our supernatural life, that part of us that will endure, has its beginnings here, in Bethlehem of Judah. Advent tells us, in fact, that it is not only Jesus who is born, but each of us as well who bears his name.

How to Use This Booklet

This booklet is intended for either individual or group use. For each day of Advent, it features the citations for and reflections on the readings and responsorial psalm of the liturgy. Each reflection begins with a summary sentence of the reading, and each day's selection of readings and reflections concludes with a question and a prayer. While some may simply want to read the Scripture passages, the reflections, and the concluding question and prayer, an extended format of daily or weekly prayer, along with suggestions for enriching the prayer experience, are offered for those who may desire a more structured approach.

If groups use this format on a weekly basis, presumably for the Sunday readings, they might find it helpful to reflect on this material during the week preceding the Sunday in question, as a way of preparing for the celebration of the Sunday Eucharist. Individuals, too, even if they are using *Living Advent* daily, will profit from considering the Sunday readings in advance.

Daily or Weekly Session Format

1. Light the appropriate candle(s) on the Advent wreath. A simple prayer, such as "Lord, help me (us) to become one with your light," might be said.

The use of the Advent wreath in the context of these sessions is strongly recommended. With its circular design and four candles, the wreath is a symbol of the eternal victory of light over dark-

ness. It also symbolizes our enlightenment in the mystery of salvation, which we hope will increase in brilliance during Advent. We Christians, empowered by the observance of the season, seek to become for all the world brighter lights of witness to the light of Christ.

2. Offer a brief prayer for enlightenment, such as "Holy Spirit, please help me (us) today to hear in these readings whatever it is you wish to say. Amen."

3. Read the first reading and its reflection.
It is strongly recommended that the readings be read aloud, even when this booklet is used individually. In a group setting, each reading and its reflection can be read by a different participant. The readings can be taken from a Bible, lectionary, or missal.

4. Pause for reflection.

5. Ask, "How do I apply this reading to my life and daily living?"
Allow sufficient time to reflect on this question and perhaps to jot some ideas down on paper. Group members might briefly share their responses and take note of any insights that they find particularly helpful. It is important, however, that participants not be made to feel that they must share their responses to any of the questions. This should always be optional. When working alone, one could take the time to write more extended and in-depth responses to the questions, using Living Advent *as a guide for journaling during the season.*

6. Read (or sing) the psalm aloud, the group responding with the antiphon.
The Psalms are liturgical songs and poems and, as such, should be read aloud or, better yet, sung, even in individual use.

7. Read the reflection on the psalm and repeat steps 4 and 5.

8. Read the second reading (Sunday only), its reflection, and repeat steps 4 and 5.

9. Read the gospel, its reflection, and once again repeat steps 4 and 5.

10. Read the closing question, aloud if in a group.
Allow sufficient time to reflect and formulate a response. Again, it may be helpful to jot some ideas down on paper. Group members might briefly share their answers.

11. The concluding prayer is said.
In a group setting, this prayer may be led by the group moderator or recited by the entire group. After this, various prayers of intercession might be offered. Group members might join hands during this time.

12. Close the session with a brief prayer, such as "Thank you, Light of the World, for hearing these prayers," and extinguish the candle(s).
At the close of the final session, group members may wish to have an informal celebration in anticipation of Christmas, with seasonal food, drink, and music. Individuals, too, may wish to find some special way to mark the heightened anticipation of Christmas in late Advent.

NOTE: For a shorter format, follow steps 1 and 2, and then read each Scripture passage and its reflection, pausing after each set. Next, read the closing question. Group members may share their responses with one another. Conclude with steps 11 and 12.

FIRST WEEK OF ADVENT

First Sunday of Advent

Reading I — Jeremiah 33:14-16

All rest safe in the justice of the Messiah raised up from the house of David. "The LORD [is] our justice."

The shoot from the house of David is "just," and Jerusalem will be known by the name "the LORD our justice." This is how the promise of God's salvation is to be fulfilled to Israel: Justice shall be established in their midst, because justice itself, that is, God himself, shall dwell among them. This justice shall be established not only in Israel but throughout all the earth.

Justice in this sense is rooted in the Hebrew word *sedek*, meaning not merely legal justice, as we might understand it today, but righteousness and right conduct. The ideal king is the Messiah, the anointed one of God, because he himself will be *sedek*, this godly righteousness. And we are his followers because we look to him as our guide to right conduct.

Justice, then, consists not in one isolated action or virtue, but in the wholehearted following of the Lord's plan for salvation. This righteousness, in fact, is salvation, God's deliverance of his people from all evil . Advent is a time for us to become rooted in justice, to grow in right conduct. It is also a time to rest secure in following the Lord who is Justice to all.

Psalm 25:4-5,8-9,10,14

We give ourselves to the Lord. "He guides the humble to justice, / he teaches the humble his way."

There are many risks involved in the spiritual life, but one of the greatest is the pride that blinds us to our own lack of spirituality. It is God who is the teacher, the guide in truth. While his paths are not always the ones we want to follow, knowing the paths that the Lord wishes us to travel requires that we give ourselves completely to him. We must be humble before God, realizing our own sinfulness. It is the humble who rely on him that he guides to justice, that he teaches his way. It is only the humble, too, who can rest their complete trust in the Lord rather than in themselves.

Advent is a season of "lifting our souls," as the psalm response states, of offering our essence. It is a season to search for the Lord's rather than our own will, a season which ends in the humility of a birth in a stable. It is a lifting which at the same time brings us to the very real earth of Bethlehem.

Reading II — 1 Thessalonians 3:12–4:2

Paul offers a prayer for love, strength, and growth in right conduct.

In Hebrew Scripture, the heart is not merely the seat of the emotions but the center of being, a representation of the entire person. In this reading, we are urged not simply to a superficial emotional response, but to let our entire being overflow with a love rooted in the strength of God. We are called to be blameless and holy and urgently exhorted to "make still greater progress."

Paul knows how important it is that each moment be dedicated to God. He knows that the coming of Christ is a reality, and the time we have now must be used to prepare for the eternity in which we hope to share. We must become one with Paul in his prayer, "May the Lord increase you....May he strengthen your hearts." We seek to put on the heart of Jesus, which has breadth and depth enough to encompass all the world in love, and so open ourselves to an increase of love for all people, as the Lord wills.

Gospel — Luke 21:25-28, 34-36

The signs of the end-times herald the coming of freedom for the righteous. "Pray constantly for the strength to escape whatever is in prospect, and to stand secure before the Son of Man."

What will enable us to stand secure in the final days to come? Nothing less than following the Lord today. It is our baptismal vocation to live and die with Christ so that we might come to share his glory. Our spirits can tend to become heavy with sin, ever more lethargic and dull. We must awake to the dawning of redeeming grace and repent. It is in so cooperating with this grace that God draws us clear of the mire of sin and into the glory of Christ.

Question: From a story told by Mother Angelica, television personality and author of books on Christian living: "An evil man was walking along and fell into the mud of sin. He was delighted and smeared himself all over with the mud. A Christian fell into the same mud of sin. He was so shocked and horrified—'Look what I've done, all this horrible mud,'—that he stayed there in the mud of sin for quite a while. Then when he finally managed to get out, he kept looking back at that mud and could barely walk along. But then a saint fell into the mud of sin. Yet the saint got right up and, trusting in the love and forgiveness of God, continued on his way." How would you apply this story to the readings for today?

Prayer: Lord, give me the humility to realize my sinfulness and the strength to change. May this Advent be a time of increase for me, a time in which I can grow as you would want. Thank you, Lord. Amen.

Monday of the First Week of Advent

Reading I — Isaiah 2:1-5

The peoples of all nations will travel to the Lord's house for instruction. He shall judge and impose peace upon all peoples. "Come, let us walk in the light of the LORD!"

Isaiah sets forth a bold vision of the messianic age, wherein we turn from our warlike ways and become the very boards, bricks, mortar, and cornerstones of the Holy City, the New Jerusalem, the dwelling place of the presence of God. We are Zion and its mount. We are the glory of God.

Yet even as we are the dwelling place of God, we, too, are sheltered by God, resting in his love, peace, and strength. As we abide in God, so might we extend his loving care to all people, especially the poor and lowly of the world. Thus, while we are housed and sheltered within God's constant love, we, at the same time, shelter and house God in a world full of inns with shuttered doors where he finds neither recognition nor admittance.

Psalm 122:1-2,3-4,4-5,6-7,8-9

"Pray for the peace of Jerusalem," the glory and the house of the Lord.

This psalm is the prayer of a pilgrim who is especially concerned with the peace and prosperity of Jerusalem. He is filled with joy to be standing within the Holy City, and because he is so near to God's dwelling place, he lays before God his heartfelt petitions.

And yet, even as the pilgrim has spoken to God, God has "spoken" to the pilgrim, insofar as God has communicated his presence to the pilgrim. So strong and embracing is this sense of God's presence that it has filled the pilgrim with rejoicing.

During Advent, we speak of the Lord's coming in glory at the end of time, of his coming in his birth, and of his coming into our hearts. As we pray, we continually open ourselves, our hearts, our lives, to God's abiding presence, that God might enter in.

Gospel — Matthew 8:5-11

"I am not worthy to have you under my roof. Just give an order and my boy will get better." Jesus commends the faith of the centurion.

In this gospel, we see the true presence of God in healing action. What was the presence of God for the centurion? It was certainly not that God be physically present. The centurion knew rather the authority of God, his power to rebuild a shattered body.

This centurion is very important, for he represents us. The centurion was a Gentile, and here we see Jesus' compassionate coming to those outside the Jewish religion. But the centurion also challenges us as Christians. He calls us to confront directly the content of our faith. What do *we* believe? Before each reception of Communion during the Mass, we echo the centurion as we say, "Lord, I am not worthy to receive you, but say only the word and I shall be healed." It is up to us to be convicted by these words, to realize what they mean in our relationship with the living God. Like the centurion, we, too, are unworthy to receive God. Like the centurion, we are called to have faith in God's healing presence. As we receive the body of Christ, we become part of the glorified Zion of the first reading, the place in which God has chosen to dwell. "Say only the word and I shall be healed." The "word" that God speaks is himself, his presence, coming as savior and healer, answering our prayers. What is our response?

Question: Today I am called to imitate the centurion in his witness of faith. What would most help me to do so?

Prayer: Lord, you have shown your love for me in more ways than I can tell. May I rejoice in you always and ever become a more thankful, trusting, faith-filled, and loving person. Thank you, Lord. Amen.

Tuesday of the First Week of Advent

Reading I — Isaiah 11:1-10

"The spirit of the LORD shall rest upon him," the messianic king-to-come who will preside over the kingdom of consummate glory.

A shoot sprouts from the stump of Jesse and a bud blossoms forth. A new creation is upon us, and the Lord of this creation, born of the line of David and Jesse, is anointed and filled with the life-giving spirit of God. He possesses wisdom and looks at the world through God's eyes. Understanding is his, and he is able to penetrate the meaning of God's word. Counsel enables him to discern God's voice so that God might guide him in his decision making. His courage in the face of difficulties is born of the strength of God. His knowledge is of God's abiding love and care. His fear of the Lord is a reverence that delights in God and the things of God, a delight so great that he cannot be deterred from fulfilling God's will for him.

Even as this spirit pervades the entire being of the Messiah, so does it pervade all that he touches. Thus, all things are made new, made whole, and brought forth into glory by the power of God. Creation is born from sin to salvation. In this transformation, we know at last a world that rests quietly in the peace and tranquillity of God. Thus, even as Advent calls us to yield to the coming of God and to be changed, so also are we called to stillness, to rest quietly in God's peace, to trust in his care.

Psalm 72:1,7-8,12-13,17

"Justice shall flourish in his time, and fullness of peace for ever." The king and his son impart blessing and salvation to all peoples.

Jesus, "the king's son," is both the peace and the justice of God. He comes as the suffering servant of God, eventually lifted up on the cross, his arms outstretched in praise of the eternal justice of God. He comes as the resurrected and glorified Lord, eternally showing forth God's justice and peace in full and resplendent bloom.

The justice and peace of Christ flow out of who he is: Son of the living God and savior of world. Our justice and peace are from Christ and flow out of our relationship with him. As the prayer over the gifts in today's liturgy states, "Lord, we are nothing without you." But with Jesus, we stand to become the sacrament of his eternal peace, his lasting justice.

We seek, then, to grow in our knowledge of and relationship with God, especially as he is revealed to us in the person of Jesus, the Word made flesh. We grow in intimacy with Jesus in our prayer, in our sharing in the life of the Church, in our relationships with our brothers and sisters in Christ. The more intimate we are with the person of Jesus, the more fully our lives, words, and actions might incarnate his justice and peace in the world.

Gospel — Luke 10:21-24

Through the Holy Spirit, God has revealed his Son not to the learned or clever, but "to the merest children." Because of this, these little ones are more blessed than the kings and prophets.

In this gospel, we see the coupling of the Spirit of God with the raising up of children to God's kingship. Jesus rejoices in the Holy Spirit because we are the children to whom the Father has been revealed, children not "qualified" but graced-filled. "Everything has been given over to me by my Father" (10:22). "Given over" is translated from the Greek word *paradidonai*, which means not simply "entrusted" but the giving over of dogma or divine revelation. We have been given some of God's knowledge, the knowledge of Father of Son, Son of Father, hidden knowledge which would never be revealed to us on our own. God's kingdom has come to us. Everything has been given by the Father to the Son—and through the Son to us. We have become part of God's family and Jesus delights in our adoption. Father, Son, and Holy Spirit unite to welcome us to them in jubilant love. We are blest indeed!

Question: Parents who have just adopted a child sometimes send out an adoption announcement. God has adopted me. What might his adoption announcement say? (Make sure this announcement shows God's great rejoicing.)

Prayer: Thank you, Lord, for making me your child. Help me to grow in the gifts of the Holy Spirit. Help me to become your peace and justice to others. And please help me to become closer to you this Advent. Thank you, Lord. Amen.

Wednesday of the First Week of Advent

Reading I — Isaiah 25:6-10

On the day of salvation, all people, freed from death and sorrow, will feast at the table of the Lord. "Let us rejoice and be glad that he has saved us!"

The end-times banquet is laid, a feast not only for the body but for the soul as well, a banquet of the redeemed, a joyous and eternal feast in the presence of God. Here, this loving God understands and allays our fears and insecurities, satisfies our hungers, anticipates and fulfills our every need. We long for this heavenly Zion, where "the Lord GOD will wipe away / the tears from all faces" (25:8).

This feast is spread on a mountaintop, the highest point in the land, a place where God was traditionally and symbolically thought to dwell. The mountaintop could be said, then, to represent the highest spiritual hopes and aspirations of the people of God. To dwell on the mountain of the Lord is to dwell with God and God-with-us, the very meaning of the word *Emmanuel*. God lifts the veil between himself and humanity, and gives the ultimate answer to all our human frailty and brokenness: his very self.

Psalm 23:1-3,3-4,5,6

"The LORD is my shepherd; I shall not want." A psalm of thanksgiving to God, who provides for all needs.

This most familiar and beloved of psalms features evocative and comforting images of tranquillity that never fail to impart a deep sense of peace and security. The compassionate strength of our Lord, leading us through the dark valley, answers a most fundamental human longing: to know that we are not alone on our journey of living and dying, but accompanied by a loving and steadfast friend. This friend, our shepherd-king, loves us more than we can realize and is abundantly present to us, so much so that our cup of blessing overflows. So great is our blessing, in fact, that it is our destiny to dwell in God's house, to rejoice in the fullness of that presence forever.

Gospel — Matthew 15:29-37

"My heart is moved with pity...." Jesus works many cures and feeds the multitude, with an abundance to spare.

Jesus had tremendous compassion for the hurts and needs of all humanity. He responded in whatever way was necessary, whether it was to heal the broken or feed the hungry. This is the mystery, the beauty, and the reassurance of the God-with-us experience: Jesus genuinely knows our needs, even better than we do, and responds in kind. We can anticipate that our messianic banquet, as prefigured in Jesus' healing and feeding, will reveal an unimaginable fullness of love, abundant enough to bring us everlasting joy.

Question: What special healing—physical, spiritual, psychological, or emotional—do I need from Jesus at this time?

Prayer: God of wisdom, enlighten me so that I may see more clearly the ways in which I need to be healed. Come to me as the good shepherd and guide me through my dark valleys. Help me surrender to you all my hurts and needs, and to trust in your compassion. Thank you, Lord. Amen.

Thursday of the First Week of Advent

Reading I — Isaiah 26:1-6

"Trust in the LORD...an eternal Rock." He humbles the mighty and lifts up the lowly.

God merits our faith in him, for he is an "eternal rock." The sublime certainty of this image, a rock unshakable by the time which brings mortal stone to ruin, heartens the soul. Even more reassuring is the end-times action of this "rock." At the end of time, we will see that reversal of position which distinguishes the kingdom of God from the kingdom of the world. The reign of justice begins. The pompous and lofty are brought down and the small in the world's view are raised to eternal kingship in heaven. Nothing shall be left of the vainglorious—their entire world is leveled even with the dust. The poor and the needy, the lowly, will become the rulers in the city of glory, and the just nation, firm in faith, will enter God's kingdom. And what is always the reward of trust in the Lord? The everlasting and unshakable peace, protection, and strength of God.

Psalm 118:1,8-9,19-21,25-27

The Lord is our refuge and strength. Thanksgiving be given to him who saves us. "Blessed is he who comes in the name of the LORD."

In this psalm, we sing exultantly of God's love and mercy and the mystery of redemption. We laud the ever-present God, who saves his people from sorrow, sin, and death. We praise the Redeemer, the blessed one, who has come in the name of the Lord, who has opened the gates of heaven to all those who have sought to take shelter in the Lord. With grateful hearts, we give thanks to the Lord for his eternal goodness.

Gospel — Matthew 7:21,24-27

"Anyone who hears my words and puts them into practice is like the wise man who built his house on rock."

The vivid image in today's gospel of the two houses—one built on rock, the other on sand—is more than an analogy. It embodies a basic truth about the spiritual life. Our faith engages us and calls us to act upon the words of the gospel, to integrate them so that they might be central to our lives and our living. In so doing, we build on a firm foundation, on the eternal rock of the first reading. Securely founded, our faith has the temperament to withstand the inevitable crises that beset us, crises that genuinely put our faith to the test: death, illness, poverty, broken relationships, substance abuse, and so on.

This isn't to suggest that our faith serves as a spiritual coping mechanism, to take the edge off our pain and suffering. Rather, our faith helps us to understand our suffering in the context of Jesus' Passion. Placed on the cross, our suffering isn't pointless, but rather is transformed into and transcended by victory, resurrection, and redemption. Even in the midst of life's storms, then, there is a certain calm, even joy, that comes from knowing that we have in our faith a sure foundation. Perhaps the words of the old Quaker hymn best express it: "No storm can shake my inmost calm, / While to that Rock I'm clinging. / Since Love is Lord of heaven and earth, / How can I keep from singing?"

Question: Think about a time in your life when you lived through a crisis. How did the rock of your faith help you to "weather the storm"?

Prayer: Loving God, empower me with your Holy Spirit, that I might put your words into practice. Give me strength, protection, and peace to persevere. Help me to trust in you, the eternal Rock. Thank you, Lord. Amen.

Friday of the First Week of Advent

Reading I — Isaiah 29:17-24

In messianic times, the Lord will right all wrongs and heal all ills. "And out of gloom and darkness, / the eyes of the blind shall see."

Isaiah speaks of more than physical sight given to the blind. He sets forth a total vision of what the kingdom of God will look like. The Just One dawns upon creation with the light of justice, ending all ills, the spiritual as well as the physical, and bringing salvation. Those who do not reverence the Lord, who fail to treat his creation with evenhanded and loving justice, who would spread darkness of any kind, are cast down.

All light and all healing come from the Just One, and he brings them to bear in the midst of our everyday darkness. It is in drawing near to him, and growing in knowledge and reverence of him, that we are made whole. We come to share in this vision of the kingdom, the light and joy of God's presence and the mystery of salvation continually unfolding in our midst.

Psalm 27:1,4,13-14

"The LORD is my light and my salvation." Wait with courage for the saving God.

This psalm of lamentation, like others of its kind, mingles a heartrending cry for God's help and protection with a confident expression of delight and hope in God's power to save. We join with the psalmist in affirming, "I believe that I shall see the bounty of the Lord / in the land of the living" (v. 13). Trust in the Lord today. He will answer our prayers. Have courage, even in the face of oppression, and wait for the Lord. He is the ever-faithful light in darkness. Know that God intends salvation for us today, that we shall see the goodness of the Lord in our own lives. He visits us with his saving power.

Gospel — Matthew 9:27-31

"Son of David, have pity on us!" Jesus heals two blind men by virtue of their faith and trust in him.

Because of the faith, trust, and confidence the blind men exhibit in their words and actions, Jesus touches their eyes and heals them. It is with the same sense of confidence, trust, and faith that we must come before God and present to him our need for healing. Like the drowning swimmer, who must trust in rather than struggle against his rescuer, we, too, must stop struggling, let go of our fears, and cooperate with God's saving help. Our healing will depend in part on the degree to which we are able to meet and give ourselves over to God's grace.

Question: In what way (or ways) in my life have I been struggling against God's saving help? Try to discern what effort it might take to resolve these struggles.

Prayer: Jesus, Son of David, have pity on me. Touch and heal me where I am wounded. Free me from fear, and help me to give myself over to and rest secure in your love. Thank you, Lord. Amen.

Saturday of the First Week of Advent

Reading I — Isaiah 30:19-21,23-26

All needs will be met abundantly by the Lord, who will heal his wounded creation. "No more will you weep."

This reading from Isaiah describes the kingdom of God's reign at the end of time. Here are enumerated the abundances provided by the Lord for his people. Rain for the seed, rich wheat, spacious meadows, fine fodder for the cattle, and flowing streams—the physical world becomes part of the goodness of God.

Also described is the ultimate paradise—a Lord who is visible, who guides our every step. No more need we ask ourselves, *Is this God's will? Am I doing the right thing?* God is present, teaching us. We can see him face to face.

This is redemption, a world without worry where physical and mental wounds are tenderly bound up and healed by the Lord. This is salvation, a Lord who not only sees and touches us but who gives us our hope-beyond-hope, the objective person of himself.

Psalm 147:1-2,3-4, 5-6

All creation is under the Lord's command as he heals and restores it. "He tells the number of the stars, / he calls each by name."

Picture the night sky in all its vastness on a clear evening. Though it is filled with stars, we know that there are even more stars beyond these, and universes beyond this universe, extending far beyond our comprehension. The majesty of the God who has set every one of these stars in place and calls each one by name inspires awe.

Truly, God is infinite might, a might that flows not from any earthly concept of power, but from a caring and unbounded love. For even as God has created the heavens and earth in all their immensity, so does he tenderly heal the wounded, the brokenhearted, the suffering.

This is the Lord whose coming we long for and anticipate, the Lord who, out of his great love, not only created all things and all peoples but also sought to share their very nature. We long for the knowledge of the Lord of creation. We long for his presence and call on his name. He comes in immense and immediate love to answer.

Gospel — Matthew 9:35–10:1,6-8

Jesus commissions his disciples to share in his ministry of healing. "The gift you have received, give as gift."

Once again, we see a caring and compassionate Savior with a heart moved to pity by our suffering, our poverty, and our ignorance of him. As we mill about, confused and unseeing, he sends us shepherds to lead us to him. By virtue of God's authority, these ministers can heal us, giving us, as a gift freely given, not only a foretaste of the complete healing that will be ours in God's kingdom but hope as well for the full realization of that kingdom. We, in turn, are asked to give freely to others what has been given to us, to minister as Jesus did, with the healing power of his presence and compassion.

Question: God calls each one of us to follow and serve in the particular circumstances of his or her life, whether as married or single, clerical, religious, or lay. At this time, how is God calling me in my state in life to minister to his creation?

Prayer: Creator God, who knows the name of every star, call me forth by name, that I might become what you would have me be, and so better serve you and others. Lord Jesus, empower me by your Holy Spirit to bring your presence, as a gift freely given, to all I encounter. In your loving care for your Church and all its ministers, send more laborers to help in your harvest. Thank you, Lord. Amen.

SECOND WEEK OF ADVENT

Second Sunday of Advent

Reading I — Baruch 5:1-9

"God is leading Israel in joy / by the light of his glory, / with his mercy and justice for company."

The Jerusalem spoken of in this reading is an end-time city, one transformed by God's own saving presence into a new creation. To be forever named by God "the peace of justice, the glory of God's worship" (5:4) means that Jerusalem actually becomes the City of God, the dwelling place of God himself. Here God establishes a complete peace and an all-encompassing justice. Here may be found the pinnacle of spiritual experience, the glory of the worship of God in his very presence.

A restored Israel returns in joy to the City of God. Israel's omnipotent leader levels mountains and fills in age-old gorges to clear the way of all hindrances. God accompanies his people, illuminating them with his radiance, giving them his mercy and justice as companions, and bringing them their greatest happiness. Restoration, peace, justice, and mercy are found in God's presence and in the worship given him.

Psalm 126:1-2,2-3,4-5,6

"The Lord has done great things for us; / we are filled with joy."

One of the signs of one who walks in the Lord's presence is joy. Spiritual life is not grim but a call to the glory of the first reading. Here the psalmist, though in exile, remembers the deliverance of the Lord as a time so wonderful that it seemed like a dream, a time filled with laughter and rejoicing.

We have been given eternal deliverance. We have a continual Hope who will comfort the sorrowing and bring the harvest to fulfillment. We must turn to the Lord, that he might relieve and refresh us in the oasis of his love. Heaven must be a place flowing with joy. Surely we should smile more often as we walk with Christ toward its gates!

Reading II — Philippians 1:4-6,8-11

With great joy, Paul anticipates "the day of Christ" (1:10), the Parousia, the time of fulfillment.

Paul's prayer for an increase in love and justice, the "things that really matter" (1:10) could be our prayer as well during Advent, especially in the face of the holiday "rush-to-buy." Love and justice aren't measured in the things of the world, in the gifts that we might receive from or give to friends and family. Rather, love is rooted in God, and Christ gives it increase in our hearts. Even as this love grows, then, so should our devotion to justice. In cultivating righteousness (the very meaning of the word *justice*) in all our words and actions, in all our dealings with others, in all our living, we cooperate and participate with Christ in bringing forth a harvest of love and justice, the harvest of the kingdom of God.

Gospel — Luke 3:1-6

John the Baptist proclaims a baptism of repentance, as was foretold by Isaiah. "Make ready the way of the Lord."

Whereas in today's first reading, the prophet Baruch speaks of God leading the faithful to glory, John the Baptist, in today's gospel, proclaims the means by which we might enter into that glory, namely, a baptism of repentance, or metanoia. Metanoia entails not only sorrow for and turning away from one's sin but also a turning toward God, a new openness to the life of God. This isn't a once-and-for-all conversion but an ongoing process, a continual placing of oneself in the presence of the forgiving Father. Each of us, in the midst of the lifeless desert of our wrongdoing, is called to metanoia, to open ourselves to the Lord who comes to lead us into glory.

Question: What am I being called to turn from this Advent and how might this help me to grow in God's love?

Prayer: Lord, bring me to metanoia and to new life. Nourish in me and in all your people the harvest of justice so needed in our time. Thank you, Lord. Amen.

Monday of the Second Week of Advent

Reading I — Isaiah 35:1-10

"The desert and the parched land will exult; / the steppe will rejoice and bloom."

In Hebrew Scripture, the desert isn't only barren land, but the place where humankind encounters God. The sparse landscape and the absence of distractions, the dryness and lack of vegetation, all render the human heart more receptive to God's word and more dependent upon God's provident mercy. Thus, the desert, for all its seeming desolation, can actually be an experience of grace and the renewal of life.

This is something of the sense we might gain from Isaiah's depiction of the flowering of the desert in the wake of springtime rains. Our human condition of sin and suffering can sometimes leave us feeling like wanderers in a dry and lifeless land. Yet, even as we parch in our desert waste and cry out to God in our need, we are startled to feel first a few drops, then a shower, then the downpour of God's love. He forgives our sins. He heals us. He gives us himself in his very presence. The seeds that lay dormant, waiting for his coming, burst into bloom, an amazing flowering of blessing and life in what we thought was worthless soil. This is divine recompense, a glorious blessing that strengthens and sustains our weakened and enfeebled faith, and renews our hope for the fullness of life yet to be revealed.

Psalm 85:9-10,11-12,13-14

The Lord will come, saving his people. Glory will dwell in our land.

Some translators believe this psalm to be a plea for rain. It is certainly a presentation of what that "rain on the desert" means to God's followers. Psalm 85 has three parts, the first two of which are not represented in today's liturgy. The first part tells how God in the past has restored Israel: "You have forgiven the guilt of your people; / you have covered all their sins" (85:3). The middle section asks that God give us life: "Show us, O LORD, your kindness, / and grant us your salvation" (85:8). The final section, today's, says, in effect, "We will see incredible things to come!"

This last section of the psalm presents an integral part of full spiritual recovery. The psalmist says, "I will hear what God proclaims!" Part of listening to and hearing God is acting on what he says. God does forgive our sins, and, having been forgiven, we show it in action. We act as children of the promise. The social virtues of kindness, truth, and justice mentioned here bespeak an acceptance of all and restore human dignity to others. This unconditional love is their birthright as God's children. We help these virtues flower to bring the incredible "glory dwelling in our land." We have been brought to life. We have been healed. It is up to us to pass this healing to all.

Gospel — Luke 5:17-26

Jesus cures a paralytic, bringing him both physical and spiritual healing. "We have seen incredible things today!"

We are amazed when a person is cured of some illness through the power of God alone. We call such healing a miracle. Because the healing we receive through the forgiveness of sins isn't always so visible and dramatic, we rarely wonder at it. Yet the entire heavenly host rejoices and the saints themselves praise in unending chorus as the Lord freely forgives the debt of the repentant sinner.

In today's gospel, Jesus forgives sins before healing physical infirmity. Sin paralyzes in a way no physical illness can. Sin is the work of the kingdom of darkness and places the sinner in eternal bondage. It is necessary that we first be freed through forgiveness before we can rise up, cleansed and praising God. Perhaps we might pause to reconsider the grace we have been given and affirm that we, too, have seen incredible things—the forgiveness of sin—yesterday, today, and always!

Question: Advent is a time of preparing the way of the Lord, for remembering Christ's birth at Bethlehem, and for anticipating his Second Coming. A daily examination of conscience is always a good idea, and might be especially helpful at this time. We might ask ourselves, *What have I done today to prepare the Lord's way? In what ways did I succeed and what opportunities did I miss?*

Prayer: Jesus, Son of the living God, have mercy on me, a sinner. During this season of joyous anticipation, help me to prepare your way, to receive you with joy, and so become a new creation. Thank you, Lord. Amen.

Tuesday of the Second Week of Advent

Reading I — Isaiah 40:1-11

Make ready the way of the Lord—and don't be afraid to proclaim the good news! God comes, a tender shepherd, to comfort and care for his flock.

Isaiah 40:1–55:13 is called the Book of Consolation, and begins, fittingly enough, with the words, "Comfort, give comfort to my people, / says your God." Those who follow God are asked to perform works of mercy, comfort, and consolation, as part of their sharing in the life of God. At the same time, however, as mortal beings, we can tend to be so fearful and hopeless in the face of our own death and the many weaknesses that beset us, that we are given to despair and inaction.

In spite of all this, we have the reassurance that "the word of our God stands forever" (40:8). We have the knowledge of God's tender care of the weak, so beautifully recounted here, to free us from fear, to give us the courage to cry out, "Here is your God!" (40:9). The time of sorrow has ended. A new creation, resplendent with God's glory, has begun. Our valleys have been filled in. Our way has been straightened. Our hope and our consolation have come in power, and we are commissioned and empowered to give his comfort to all.

Psalm 96:1-2,3,10,11-12,13

All creation exults in a joyous hymn before the God of salvation, who comes in strength to rule with justice. "Sing to the LORD a new song."

Christmas is the season of the carol. These most popular of all hymns, traversing almost all Christian traditions, unify us and give us a special gift of beauty and melody in this season of joy. Christmas carols warm and uplift our hearts. The singing at Christmas services rings out with a power and rejoicing not found in the rest of the year.

Psalm 96 is like the consummate carol. All creation resounds with song in praise of the coming of God. All peoples and nations, the heavens and the earth, the sea and its contents, everything praises God in glorious chorus. The strong King comes, ruling with justice, and the universe exults. To herald the advent of this king is to herald the advent of salvation. Of how many earthly rulers might this be said? How many earthly rulers are so worthy of their subjects' trust and confidence? This divine King certainly merits a new song, expressing the triumph of God's new reign.

Gospel — Matthew 18:12-14

"It is no part of your heavenly Father's plan that a single one of these little ones shall ever come to grief."

The shepherd of Jesus' parable has such compassion for his sheep that it is impossible for him to ignore the one who is at risk of being lost, even though ninety-nine of his flock are secure. He must go to the "little one" who may be hurt, trapped, or in anguish.

We, as the Lord's disciples, are called to love with his tenderness, his compassion, with his very heart. We are called to share in his concern for the lost sheep, to help find them and bring them home, back to the glory of God. As such, we cannot ignore those who stray from the fold. Even the greatest sinner is a "little one," worthy of our most vigilant and solicitous care.

Question: In what ways might the Lord be calling me to care for his lost sheep?

Prayer: Lord, may I never cease to praise you for the great love you have shown me in seeking me out and saving me from my sin. Help me to reach out to others with love and concern, especially those who may be lost and confused. Thank you, Lord. Amen.

Wednesday of the Second Week of Advent

Reading I — Isaiah 40:25-31

"They that hope in the LORD will renew their strength, / they will soar as with eagles' wings."

The ancient Israelites believed that after the eagle molted, its strength was renewed. When a bird molts, it sheds its feathers so as to be ready for new growth. During Advent, then, it is our calling to cast off anything that might rob us of our hope and stand in the way of our own renewal, most especially any impatience or despair in the face of our weakness and brokenness. We seek to open ourselves to a gracious God who comes to offer us hope that we might be borne aloft on his love. He knows us, and all our weakness and discouragement as well, and yet, is always faithful to us. This steadfast love is the source of our hope, and even as we hope in God, he sustains and strengthens us.

Psalm 103:1-2,3-4,8,10

"Bless the LORD, O my soul." The psalmist thanks the Lord for his great and everlasting goodness.

Today's psalm calls us to bless and thank the Lord because he has healed us and crowned us with compassion. In Hebrew Scripture, a blessing conferred life from God, bringing new power and strength to the person blessed. We bless God in this psalm because God has blessed us with us new birth. Thus, blessing has a circular movement, from God to us and from us to God, with more abundant blessings being realized as we lift an increasingly thankful heart to our generous God. Understood as such, all things might ultimately be seen as blessing from God.

Gospel — Matthew 11:28-30

Jesus invites his followers to the rest and refreshment that he alone can give.

The events of our lives often discourage us. We walk with heads bowed in what seems to be an increasingly troubled world. We become aware of our own spiritual poverty, destitute in our particular sufferings and sorrows.

In the midst of all this, Jesus invites us to the rest and refreshment which is himself. He invites us, as his followers, to learn from him, to be formed in his spirit of humility and gentleness, to take on his yoke, the law of love.

It was in his gentleness and humility that Jesus took our humanity on himself and brought his divine life to bear on us. He has brought us salvation. He has raised us higher than any eagle might soar. Thus, gentleness and humility bring healing and wholeness, and it is in our own gentleness and humility of heart that we will encounter him, faithful and compassionate.

We are called in a special way during Advent to become more gentle and humble. It is a time of refreshment in which our burdens are lifted so that, without pride or arrogance, we might carry God's love into the world.

Question: Pride and hardness of heart leave me burdened and imprisoned within myself. In what ways is the Lord calling me to his gentleness, meekness, and humility?

Prayer: Jesus, meek and humble of heart, make my heart like yours. Forgive my sins of pride and arrogance. Lift my burdens, renew me in your love, and give me the courage to help lift the burdens of others. Thank you, Lord. Amen.

Thursday of the Second Week of Advent

Reading I — Isaiah 41:13-20

"Fear not, O worm Jacob, / O maggot Israel." The Lord will redeem us, strengthening us and supplying our every need.

Throughout history, Israel's relationship with God has been personal and familial. It is a relationship whose intimacy may be likened to that which exists between child and parent, sister and brother, or wife and husband. Hence, the words *worm* and *maggot* are not to be understood as terms of disgust or contempt, but rather as terms of endearment, the sort of pet names that a loving father might address to the child nestled in his lap.

It is with this same sense that the Hebrew word *go'el*—translated in the lectionary as "redeemer"—is used in this passage. *Go'el* not only denotes "one who saves" but connotes a familial bond as well, a relationship so close and loving that the redeemer in question cannot fail to respond to the needs of those who are in need of redemption.

God first revealed himself as *go'el,* as our father-redeemer, in the covenant of family love, in the exodus event. There he led his own out of the fear and oppression of slavery into freedom. In Advent, we are called to be part of a new exodus. In remembering Christ's first coming and anticipating his *Parousia,* we celebrate the journey of faith that we have undertaken. God the father, through Christ his son, leads us forth in joy and confidence to the kingdom, to waters of life, to a complete transformation of mind, soul, and body.

Psalm 145:1,9,10-11,12-13

All the works of God should praise the glorious King of salvation. "Let your faithful ones bless you."

It's hard at times to believe in God's complete, unconditional and eternal love. Yet, as today's psalm tells us, this is the God who loves us: a God of great kindness, patience, compassion, mercy, and might, a God whose faithfulness, glory, and dominion are everlasting. Although he has intimate knowledge of us and our sins, he also bears toward us an intimate and infinite love. It is a father's love. It is a mother's love. It is a child's love. It is a lover's love. It is all love.

Such a love requires a response from us. This psalm exhorts us to respond to God with praise, to bless his name, to extol his incredible goodness, love, and compassion. It is in the happiness and joy that comes from knowing God's love for us that we seek to commit to God our entire being—body, soul, mind, and heart—in praise of his love. Then it is that our true life in his kingdom begins, to know that God rejoices to love us, and we rejoice to love him.

Gospel — Matthew 11:11-15

"History has not known a man born of woman greater than John the Baptizer." Yet the least born into the kingdom of God is greater than he.

Jesus' coming is the climax of all human history, the crossroads where time and eternity intersect. God has "broken into" time, ushering in his kingdom. Jesus Christ unifies the glory of God with our often-abject humanity, so transforming us that even the least of this kingdom will be mightier than one such as John the Baptist. Truly, nothing will ever be the same again.

Yet, even as the kingdom has been established in our midst, we are watching and waiting for its fulfillment. In Flannery O'Connor's novel *The Violent Bear It Away,* whose title is based on Matthew 11:12, today's gospel reading, her protagonist comes to realize that his hunger is that of the prophets, "who would wander in the world, strangers from that violent country where the silence is never broken except to shout the truth." Like John the Baptist, we are called to a prophetic role, to be penitent and purified, and to proclaim the kingdom. We are called to burn with passion and to shout out the truth. We are called as well to be consumed with hunger for Jesus, a hunger so great that nothing except the Lord himself will ever completely fill our emptiness.

Question: The example of John the Baptist challenges me to work passionately for God's kingdom. What is my response?

Prayer: Lord, anoint me as your prophet. Give me the fire of your Holy Spirit to burn away my weaknesses and proclaim your salvation. Let me hunger for you more than anything else. Thank you so much for your love. Amen.

Friday of the Second Week of Advent

Reading I — Isaiah 48:17-19

"If you would hearken to my commandments, / your prosperity would be like a river, / and your vindication like the waves of the sea."

Today's first reading refers indirectly to two men of faith who sought to follow God's will for them, namely, Moses, who received the Ten Commandments, and Abraham, who was promised descendants as numerous as grains of sand. The stories of Moses and Abraham illustrate the truth that, in listening to, learning from, and obeying the will of God, however difficult this may be, one is brought to salvation. We are called to follow their example, to open ourselves to the working of God's grace so that we, too, might come to know salvation. Though our trials may be great, our reward, like theirs, will be unending, flowing like a river and as ceaseless as the waves of the sea.

Psalm 1:1-2,3,4,6

"The LORD watches over the way of the just, / but the way of the wicked vanishes."

Those who follow the Lord's way are promised eternal joy. Great happiness fills those who avoid sin and delight in God's law. Following in the way of a loving God does not lead to a legalistic misery but to a deep-rooted happiness, "like a tree / planted near running water" (v. 3), nourished and protected and set apart in the oasis of God's love.

We are called not to obey God's law unthinkingly, but rather to meditate on it day and night. This is as much to say that we are called to an ongoing personal discernment of God's will for us. We are asked to consider not only the wrong we may have done but also the right we may have left undone.

Despite our sin, we are not without hope. The psalm response reminds us: "Those who follow you, Lord, will have the light of life." Jesus said, "I am the light of the world. Whoever follows me will not walk in darkness, but will have the light of life" (John 8:12). Jesus stands before us, his presence illuminating our path. We follow him into everlasting light.

Gospel — Matthew 11:16-19

One cannot live to please one's critics. "Time will prove where wisdom lies."

One of the greatest challenges for the Christian is discovering what God wants done. (An even greater challenge is doing it!) This is because God's law is not made up of absolutes. The law of love frees us, and yet is more than a set of regulations. Thus we see John the Baptist and Jesus doing, in the eyes of the world, exactly the opposite. John fasts, Jesus feasts. Both are criticized for their actions, but both follow God's plan. Time and eternity have proven their wisdom.

Christian's are everlasting nonconformists, continually at odds with the standards of the world, and the world resents their differentness. The children depicted playing in the squares are probably playing at marriages, where there would be dancing, and funerals, at which there would be wailing. They are highly insulted that their companions refuse to join in their imitation of life. Christian's are called to turn their backs on the imitations of life. True life is with God. True life is unity with the Life and the Light. True life has Jesus as its center and is proven by our actions. Christ says to us here, "What my reputation is doesn't matter. I am willing to be judged by the consequence of my deeds. Are you?"

Question: Jesus should be at the center of my life. In what areas do I need to yield to him more fully?

Prayer: Lord, help me to yield to you, that you might bring me into conformity with your will. Make of me the person you want me to be. Fill me with your faith, hope, and love, and give me the courage to stand up and be counted as a Christian. Thank you, Lord. Amen.

Saturday of the Second Week of Advent

Reading I — Sirach 48:1-4,9-11

"How awesome are you, Elijah! Whose glory is equal to yours?"

Elijah the prophet lived nine centuries before Christ. His life stands as a tribute to the power of the word of God, demonstrating that God fulfilled his promises, took care of his people, and answered prayer. By the end of his life, Elijah had been fed miraculously by ravens; had multiplied food for a widow and brought her dead son back to life; had seen his sacrifices consumed by fire as a sign of the Lord's favor; and had witnessed his enemies struck by the lightning of the Lord as they came to arrest him. Rather than dying, he left the world in a chariot of fire, and it was believed that he would return again, as an augury of the coming of the Messiah.

Yet Elijah stood forth not only as a man of signs and wonders but also as a man who heard the true voice of God. In one incident (1 Kings 19ff), Elijah stands upon a mountain, waiting to hear the voice of the Lord. The Lord speaks to him, not in a mighty wind, not in an earthquake, not in a raging fire, but rather in a gentle breeze. This is the breath of the Holy Spirit, touching us, not in destruction, but in intimacy, speaking God's word with the gentleness that can come only from one so near to us that he might whisper in our ear. Elijah witnesses to the nearness of God, both in great wonders and in the whisperings of the spirit. The Lord is as close to us as our own heart. Listen for his voice.

Psalm 80:2-3,15-16,18-19

"Rouse your power, / and come to save us."

In the past, God had guided and protected Israel, his chosen people, and in this psalm, Israel pleads for his help once again. Suffering makes one remember God's past goodness and challenges one to turn to and rely on God alone. In the poverty of pain, there is nothing left but God's love. When all the props are removed, one is more receptive to what God has to say. Israel, in her suffering, has turned to God in prayer and hope.

During Advent, we, too, turn to God in prayer and hope. In our weakness and suffering, we are opened to receive God's Word, to celebrate the mystery of the Incarnation, the Word made flesh. We remember that God comes as the Son of Man, as one of us, to suffer with us and for us. We remember a baby, weak and lowly, born in a stable. And yet we rejoice, for in the weakness of this baby, we see the Lord who has come in power to save us. We rejoice, for even now, this mystery of salvation is at work within us and brought to fulfillment in our midst.

Gospel — Matthew 17:10-13

The Son of Man will suffer as John did.

In today's gospel, Jesus refers to one of the hallmarks of the Son of Man, namely, suffering. The suffering of the prophets and John the Baptist foreshadows Jesus' own suffering. Christ would not be recognized and would have to suffer, even as they did.

Our knowledge of the sufferings of Christ is an important inheritance, for Scripture tells us that our own sufferings are united with those of the Son of Man, to bring to fulfillment his work of redemption. Paul says, "Now I rejoice in my sufferings for your sake, and in my flesh I am filling up what is lacking in the afflictions of Christ on behalf of his body which is the church" (Colossians 1:24). Whatever we do and whatever we endure, whether voluntary or involuntary, can be offered for the love of God and for the salvation of the world. Whether young or old, rich or poor, strong or weak, sick or well, regardless of one's state in life, all are Christ's associates in sanctification.

Question: God gives me the opportunity to help him in his work of redemption. What suffering am I willing to endure, what penance and good works might I offer today, for the salvation of the world?

Prayer: Lord, help me to offer all that I do and all that I might suffer for the salvation of the world. Help me to hear your voice always, wherever I am and whatever I do. May I always realize how very close to me you are and how completely you love me. Thank you, Lord. Amen.

THIRD WEEK OF ADVENT

Third Sunday of Advent

Reading I — Zephaniah 3:14-18

Israel is called to rejoice, for her salvation is coming, God dwelling in her midst. "He will rejoice over you with gladness, / and renew you in his love."

Zephaniah presents us with an astonishing image: God, incredibly joyful because of *us*, sings and, according to some translations of this passage, even dances with elation. The Lord exults in his people the same way a bridegroom exults in his bride, with a love that finds excitement and jubilation in the very presence of the beloved.

How can we return a glorious love like this? The reading suggests shouting and singing. Yet it is almost as if sound is not enough—a God in our midst who loves us so much that he sings and dances! The renewing power of Emmanuel, God-with-us, dwelling in our midst, brings us blessing beyond our greatest hope and imagining. He brings the life which is himself and the joy which knows no end.

Psalm — Isaiah 12:2-3,4,5-6

"Sing praise to the LORD for his glorious achievement; / let this be known throughout all the earth."

This canticle calls us to acclaim and proclaim God's name and make his deeds known to all nations, to make his glorious achievements known throughout all the earth. Our shouts of exultation are not merely for ourselves, our friends, our families, or the members of our church, but for all to hear. God, our strength and our courage, empowers us that we might openly rejoice in and give witness to our faith. The Lord, our fountain of salvation, rescues us from our fear and timidity. The Holy Spirit fills us, that we might joyfully bring Christ to all the world.

Reading II — Philippians 4:4-7

"Rejoice in the Lord always! I say it again. Rejoice!"

When faced with the difficulties and trials of our human condition—death, suffering, and our own inhumanity to one another—how can we rejoice always, let alone find peace? *Shalom*, the Hebrew word for "peace," signifies more than mere tranquillity and the absence of war. In some instances, *shalom* is almost synonymous with salvation. It is a sign of the fulfillment of God's covenant promises, a peace which is truly God's own, a deep union and harmony with his will.

It is our God's nearness to us that gives us this lasting peace, this harmony with the will of God that stands guard over our hearts. Unselfishly, without anxiety, and in grateful prayer, we should rejoice in God's presence and in following his will. Then the *shalom* of God, beyond all understanding, will shield us from harm.

Gospel — Luke 3:10-18

John exhorts the people to prepare themselves for the judgment of the Lord by reforming their lives. "His winnowing-fan is in his hand to clear his threshing floor and gather the wheat into his granary, but the chaff he will burn in unquenchable fire."

"What ought we to do?" Those who ask this of John are told to straighten their lives, becoming honest, gentle, and generous. John stresses that he is not the Messiah, and that the Messiah is superlatively better than himself. While John baptizes in water, the Messiah will baptize with the power of the Holy, the power by which the Church will flare into being in the Pentecost event. The image that follows of the winnowing of the wheat is most apt. Wind is the chief agent in winnowing.

Threshed grain is tossed into the air. The useless chaff is carried away by wind, while the heavier wheat falls to the floor to be harvested. To prepare ourselves for the eternal harvest, it is necessary to let the wind of the Spirit separate our wheat from our chaff and to reform our lives.

Question: A rejoicing God comes into our midst, offering us salvation. In preparation for his coming, which elements of my life are the "wheat" that I should retain, and which are the "chaff" that I should discard?

Prayer: Lord God, give me your *shalom*, the abiding peace of living in harmony with your will. Send forth your spirit to blow and burn away my chaff and inflame me with the joy of salvation. Thank you, Lord. Amen.

Monday of the Third Week of Advent

(N.B. *If today is December 17 or 18, omit these readings and reflections, and use those given for the late Advent weekdays, pp. 49-64).*

Reading I — Numbers 24:2-7,15-17

The seer Balaam speaks of the rise of Israel and her vindication against her foes. "A star shall advance from Jacob, / and a staff shall rise from Israel."

The story of Balaam, the sage who spoke this prophecy, is an interesting one. Balak, the king of Moab, reigning thirteen centuries before the birth of Christ, asked Balaam to curse (that is, to cast a spell against) Israel, to render her powerless in battle against the Moabites. Balaam, however, can utter only what the Lord enjoins him to pronounce, a blessing upon Israel. Three times Balak asks Balaam to curse Israel, and three times Balaam can speak only blessing. When an angry Balak orders the seer to depart with no pay, Balaam proclaims his last message from the Lord, in which the star advances from Jacob and the staff rises from Israel. Balaam announces not just victory, but a messianic kingship!

Balaam admirably fulfills his role as prophet. As God imparts wisdom without stint, Balaam responds to this generosity with a total commitment to speak God's word without compromise. Even when, like so many other prophets, he is reviled rather than honored for his integrity, Balaam remains faithful to the truth. To know and speak God's truth is recompense enough.

Psalm 25:4-5,6-7,8-9

"Your ways, O Lord, make known to me."

Even though God has revealed so much to us, both through his inspired Word and through his Word made flesh, our knowledge of God remains imperfect. We plead in the words of the psalm response, "Teach me your ways, O Lord." Our hope lies in the mercy of our Savior, who, in grace, "shows sinners the way" (v. 8), revealing and returning us to the right path.

The psalmist declares that it is the humble who learn God's way and come to justice. Yet how frequently pride bars our way to God, keeping us from repentance and from knowing God. Our prayer should be for humility, that we might be emptied of all that is inessential, and so be filled with that which alone is essential, God himself.

Gospel — Matthew 21:23-27

The chief priests and elders try to ensnare Jesus with a question but are caught in their own trap.

In this dramatic scene, we see the chief priests and elders caught on the horns of a dilemma. If they acknowledge that John's authority comes from God, they must acknowledge that Jesus, whom John pointed to as the one who was to come, is the Messiah. Yet if they refuse to acknowledge the authority of John, they may incur the wrath of the people, who believe John to be an authentic prophet.

Their quibbling reply to Jesus' question is not without significance. God gives the chief priests and elders the opportunity to speak and attest to the truth. Fearing the displeasure of the people, they refuse to reply at all. In their culpability, arrogance, and pride, they fall into their own trap. They have publicly admitted their lack of wisdom and authority. It is Jesus alone who possesses the full wisdom and authority of God.

Question: By virtue of my baptism, I am called to proclaim God's truth with courage and conviction, in all that I say and do. How have I been called to this in the past, and how am I being called to it now?

Prayer: Lord, free me from pride so that I may humbly seek to do your will. Give me the wisdom, courage, and strength to proclaim your truth. Thank you, Lord. Amen.

Tuesday of the Third Week of Advent

(N.B. *If today is December 17 or 18, omit these readings and reflections, and use those given for the late Advent weekdays, pp. 49-64).*

Reading I — Zephaniah 3:1-2,9-13

A faithful remnant, "a people humble and lowly," will come to know the saving power of God.

Israel in the time of Zephaniah was a nation of the materially poor. Wealth was concentrated in the hands of the few, leaving little opportunity or likelihood for anyone else to become monetarily rich. The "chosen" poor were the faithful who placed all their desire and trust in God, having nothing else on which they might depend. Aware of their great need for God, they had abandoned themselves entirely to their Creator, and having thus chosen, they, in turn, became spiritually "rich." God always recognizes the true worth of these poor and lowly ones, regardless of their race or nation. For the faith and confidence they have shown, God visits them with salvation and raises them on high.

Psalm 34:2-3,6-7,17-18,19,23

The Lord saves the poor, those who are brokenhearted and crushed in spirit.

Israel's history is the story of the poor, those who have given themselves totally to the Lord, who rejoice in doing his will and who wait for and trust in the saving power of God. Israel could anticipate that, as she deferred to God's will, he would rescue and redeem her, raising her up in deliverance. Israel rejoices, for she knows that God will come to save his people, bringing great blessing for those who are ready to meet him.

Our thankfulness and rejoicing should be at least as great as Israel's. We, too, should "glory in the LORD" (v. 3). Jesus' life and ministry epitomizes and fulfills the history of Israel. He was the poor and lowly chosen of God who endured suffering and death, even death on the cross. For this, he has been brought to exaltation, a raising-up which he shares with us. We pray for and anticipate this new life, preparing ourselves to meet him with rejoicing when he comes to reign as the resurrected and glorified Lord of life.

Gospel — Matthew 21:28-32

Those who do the will of God will be first in his kingdom.

Who enters into the kingdom of God? As we have seen in today's first reading and responsorial psalm, it is the poor, those who have nothing else on which to rely but the mercy of God, and who seek to do God's will in everything. According to today's gospel, even those whose first inclination is not to do the will of God may become as these poor whom God visits with salvation. Those who have heard the message of John, who rely on God's mercy, repent of their sin, and seek to live in the holiness to which they have been called, will enter into God's kingdom. Past sinfulness is no barrier. The kingdom is given not to the sanctimonious, to the "eldest sons," the chief priests and elders, who only pay lip service to the will of God, but to the "second sons," the repentant sinners, those who now and in the future sincerely follow the Lord.

Question: How might I alter my conduct so as to follow God's will more faithfully?

Prayer: Lord, you have given me hope that, through your forgiveness, I might enter your kingdom, regardless of my past sinfulness. Call me to true repentance for my sins. Forgive me and set me free from any barrier that would keep me from doing your will. Thank you, Lord. Amen.

Wednesday of the Third Week of Advent

(N.B. *If today is December 17 or 18, omit these readings and reflections, and use those given for the late Advent weekdays, pp. 49-64*).

Reading I — Isaiah 45:6-8,18,21-25

"In the LORD shall be the vindication and the glory / of all the descendants of Israel."

The Hebrew word for justice is *sedek*. *Sedek* originally was understood in legal terms, in that one was considered "just" when not guilty of crime. Hence, the righteous were those who obeyed the law. As the term developed over time, *sedek* additionally came to connote right conduct in general, and finally reached its fullest meaning when it came to be understood as salvation or deliverance.

It is this ultimate meaning of *sedek,* that of victory, salvation, and deliverance, that brings us the most joyous tidings. In today's readings, justice descends like rain, making salvation to blossom from the earth. We may trust in the Lord of the universe, who comes with the justice of salvation, bringing vindication and glory and delivering all the descendants of Israel.

Psalm 85:9-10,11-12,13-14

"Justice shall walk before him, / and salvation, along the way of his steps."

In the late fourth century A.D., Saint Jerome endeavored to translate the entire Bible into Latin, producing what came to be known as the Vulgate. Today's responsorial antiphon, "Let the clouds rain down the Just One, and the earth bring forth a savior," is based on the Vulgate rendering of this text from Isaiah 45 (today's first reading) rather than the *New American Bible.* In his translation, Jerome gave this text a more messianic thrust by translating *justice* as Just One, and *salvation* as savior. Justice and salvation are thus personified, even incarnated, in the figure of the Messiah, whom, in the light of our faith, we know to be Jesus.

Today's liturgy, then, is enriched by a Church tradition that emphasizes Christ as the fulfillment of the messianic promise. We, too, have been enriched through our knowledge of this Just One. Jesus is justice and peace. He is kindness and truth. He reveals to us in his own person the very meaning of this psalm. These words are translated into his being. We know our salvation personally. He has walked among us and shown us his way.

Gospel — Luke 7:18-23

"The poor have the good news preached to them."

Today's first reading told us that "only in the LORD are just deeds and power" (Isaiah 45:24). Jesus here demonstrates just deeds and power, proving him to be Lord. Each of those suffering from physical illness is healed, but even more, as a supreme sign of salvation, the poor have the good news preached to them.

The poor (that is, the lowly who have given up all to follow God's will) long intensely for God. The good news that comes to them, that the Just One is here, that God's kingdom has been established, brings them wholeness in a way that mere physical healings cannot. They are trans-figured. They become part of the throng of the redeemed, marching into the glory long foretold by the prophets.

The poor progress into glory precisely because they have centered themselves upon God in trust and faith, knowing that his kingdom is not of this world. Those who expect an earthly kingdom will find Jesus to be a stumbling block. They will be scandalized at the thought of total com-mitment and abandonment to Jesus and his way. The poor, on the other hand, find no stumbling block in Jesus, but rather the way to salvation.

Question: The poor, the lowly, and the broken, those who had nothing on which to rely but the saving power of God: it was to these that Jesus came, preaching the good news. Looking back over my own personal history, how has God been able to effect good and healing from the difficulties and losses that I have known?

Prayer: Lord, all creation is part of your plan for salvation. Help me to long for your coming, and to prepare for it by trusting in you, rather than in the things of the world. Thank you, Lord. Amen.

Thursday of the Third Week of Advent

(N.B. *If today is December 17 or 18, omit these readings and reflections, and use those given for the late Advent weekdays, pp. 49-64*).

Reading I — Isaiah 54:1-10

"My love shall never leave you." The Lord has called Jerusalem back to himself. She, who was like a barren wife, shall become abundantly fruitful, for she is wedded to God, whose covenant is eternal.

God has made an enduring covenant with his people, calling us to a union with himself that is as close as that between husband and wife, a melding that will make us one with our Redeemer. Tenderly and com-passionately, then, God strives to melt our hearts, that we might respond to his love with that same tenderness and compassion.

"Fear not," Isaiah tell us. In this, we hear the angels' voices as they reassure both Mary and the shepherds. Those whom the Lord loves and who love him in return give birth to God in their very being. God's union with Israel brought forth both the child and the Church. God's union with us, at once collective and individual, brings his own Mystical Body to bear within each of us and among all of us.

We, in turn, are in intimate communion not only with him but with all who love him. In the tremendous abundance of this ever-giving love, we, as Church, are given increase and the freedom to open our arms to all the world, to all God's creation. As the prophet exhorts us, "Enlarge the space of your tent," for many are the children of the Lord.

Psalm 30:2,4,5-6,11-12,13

The psalmist thanks and praises God for the gift of salvation. "At nightfall, weeping enters in, / but with the dawn, rejoicing."

This psalm is a prayer of thanksgiving for the healing of a serious illness. Just as in the previous reading the barren were healed and made fruitful, so here does darkness turn to dawn and anguish to ecstasy as life flourishes anew. As the psalmist is brought up from the nether world and drawn clear of death, his joy is such that his mourning is turned into dancing.

Illness, pain, or whatever our "darkness" might be, is turned to light and joy as God visits us with his saving power. We are reminded that God is there beside us, with power and hope, to heal and restore us. Salvation comes to us daily through the grace of God. There is an old Christmas carol that goes, "Tomorrow shall be my dancing day." Tomorrow will always be the dancing day of those who look to God as their Savior and wait on his saving power.

Gospel — Luke 7:24-30

"I send my messenger ahead of you, / to prepare your way before you."

Who John *is not* tells us something of who John *is*. John is not a reed swayed by the wind. He is a man of permanent conviction. John is not a luxuriously dressed member of a royal household. As a prophet, his clothing is ascetic and recalls that of Elijah. Those journeying to the desert to see John, if they are sincere, expect to see a prophet who will proclaim to them the word of the Lord.

Yet John is, as Jesus says, something more than a prophet. He is the one who, as indicated in Luke's citation from the prophet Malachi, prepares the way for the coming of the God who purifies and refines his people. He is the herald of the kingdom-to-come. So great beyond all imagining is this kingdom that even a man such as John, greater than all those who have gone before him, is as nothing compared to the least of its subjects. It is a kingdom of the redeemed, the saved, the purified, and the healed. It is a kingdom of everlasting life.

During these days of preparation for the coming of God and his kingdom, John's voice is ever in our ears. Repent, he says. Turn to God and begin again. The Pharisees and lawyers, by refusing John's baptism of metanoia, block God's plan for their own salvation. They will not bend to acknowledge their God and Redeemer. In their rigidity, they lack faith and will not listen to John. In their tragic self-regard, they ignore both the compassionate King and his vast kingdom of merciful love.

Question: Even as God embraces me with his love, so does he call me to embrace all the world with that love. To whom can I bring God's love today?

Prayer: Lord, you love me so much. How can I ever repay you? Give me a heart that turns to you in repentance for my sins. Help me to reflect your love in the way I love others. Thank you, Lord, for your mercy and forgiveness. Amen.

Friday of the Third Week of Advent

(N.B. *If today is December 17 or 18, omit these readings and reflections, and use those given for the late Advent weekdays, pp. 49-64).*

Reading I — Isaiah 56:1-3,6-8

The Lord's house shall be called "a house of prayer for all peoples," for the Lord welcomes all who follow his law.

The words "house of prayer," which are frequently written over the doors of synagogues, were given new emphasis in the documents of Vatican II. The Council stressed that the Church is the people of God, living stones built up into a house of prayer, the temple of the Body of Christ. Our foundation is the rock of obedience to God's law, and we are fitted together with Jesus the High Priest as capstone and head.

As we minister, love, and become servants in Christ's image, our spiritual home grows. As we are unified with others who serve and worship in Christ's name, the Church becomes an edifice that embraces all peoples in all places, making the world a temple consecrated to God. We anticipate that, in the end-times, all those who are faithful to God's covenant, who are gathered into the Lord's house of prayer, shall join in an unending and glorious liturgy of joyful praise.

Psalm 67:2-3,5,7-8

God's blessing extends to all nations. "May God's face shine upon us."

God instructed Moses that Aaron should bless Israel with these words: "The LORD bless you and keep you! / The LORD let his face shine upon you, / and be gracious to you!" (Numbers 6:24-25) The spirit of this blessing permeates this psalm, and as the previous reading told us, God's blessing is extended not only to Israel but to all nations. The shining face of God is so bright that it cannot be limited to one people, but must illuminate the world.

Evangelization really begins with walking in the light of the Lord. All who have known this radiance must carry it in covenant faithfulness to others. As we follow Christ, his face becomes our own. Others, in looking at us, behold him. We become part of that royal priesthood to which Aaron was called. We lift up the Lord for the world to see and offer him to all.

Gospel — John 5:33-36

John the Baptist testifies to the glory of Jesus, and Jesus proclaims it in his own works, showing that it is the Father who sent him.

The lamp "set aflame and burning bright" (5:35), representing the person of John the Baptist, may be likened to those that burn constantly in churches and temples to signify the presence of God. Certainly, John's testimony is a sign pointing to the coming Messiah, but even greater is the witness given by the works of Jesus. As these works bring physical and spiritual healing, shattering the darkness of pain and ending the night of sin, they demonstrate that Jesus himself is Emmanuel, the very presence of our saving God dwelling in our midst.

Moreover, these works are a visible sign of Jesus' relationship to the Father, not only proving Christ's origins but also showing, in the Son, what the Father is like. The face that shines forth is one of compassion, a compassion actively engaged, as in Genesis, in the creation of light and enlightenment.

Question: Light, light-bearers, and the lucidity of right conduct and love irradiate today's readings. We have seen that the coming of God is one that brightens all nations and all things. How can I testify to the light today so as to brighten my world?

Prayer: Lord, heal me of my own sinfulness. I repent of my sins and pray that you help me walk in and carry your light. Make of me the kind of temple and house of prayer that you desire. Thank you, Lord. Amen.

LATE ADVENT

Fourth Sunday of Advent

Reading I — Micah 5:1-4

The messianic king "shall stand firm and shepherd his flock...he shall be peace."

Micah asserts that the messianic king shall be not only a strong and compassionate shepherd but also *peace itself*. This is a very strong statement since, as was noted in the reflection for last Sunday's second reading, the Hebrew word for peace, *shalom*, connotes a state of perfect unity with God and with his will. Such a king would be the fulfillment of all the hopes of God's people, since this peace, coupled with strength and compassionate care, could only be fully realized in the coming of God himself. Jesus, then, is the fulfillment of Micah's prophecy. With his coming, we are rooted in his peace and come to know his compassionate care.

Psalm 80:2-3,15-16,18-19

The psalmist prays God to come in power and save his people. "Give us new life, and we will call upon your name."

Our salvation is always a matter of grace. It is God's grace that enables us to turn to him, that gives us new life, and that inspires us to call upon his name. In this psalm, and during all of Advent, we pray for the grace of metanoia, that we might turn again to God and ask his forgiveness. We pray that we have the power and the courage to be freed of all that separates us from God, that we may no longer withdraw from him. We seek to know that the grace of God rests upon us as our Savior is born within our hearts. We pray that our actions are such that this birth may take place and that Christ may reign within us.

Reading II — Hebrews 10:5-10

"I have come to do your will, O God."

"Thy will be done." These are some of the hardest and the easiest words to say to God. They are the hardest because God's way is sometimes difficult and not of our own choosing. They are some of the easiest words to say because they take the pressure off. We don't have to do it all ourselves. God will help and we can't go wrong in doing what God wants us to do. Jesus' following of God's will sets the pattern, showing us the freedom won through obedience.

Gospel — Luke 1:39-45

"Blessed is she who trusted that the Lord's words to her would be fulfilled."

Mary goes to Elizabeth, both to help her and to receive her counsel, and is greeted with a proclamation of the glories to come. The babe in Elizabeth's womb leaps with joy, just as King David had danced with joy before the Ark of the Covenant, the ark that housed the presence of God. He has come, the king of ages! Elizabeth calls Mary "blessed among women," blessed because God dwells within her, blessed because she had trusted that God would fulfill all his promises to her.

Advent is a time of decision. We know all that God has promised us in his holy Word. We must respond to these promises with trust. Without trust, we are left standing outside the stable, bereft of hope, scanning a darkened sky for a star that never comes. Once more, then, we must affirm that Jesus is our Lord, trust in his power to save us, and prepare him a new and special resting place within a chastened heart.

Question: Each of us and all of us, as members of Christ's Body, are a living sacrament, bearing Jesus' light and life into the world. In what ways might I become more like Christ for others?

Prayer: Lord, show me your face and help me to draw closer to you. Fill me with your life, that I may be a sacrament of your presence to others. Help me to trust in your promise, preparing my heart to receive you in the coming celebration of your birth. Thank you, Lord. Amen.

Late Advent Weekday: December 17

Reading I — Genesis 49:2, 8-10

The heritage of Judah will last forever.

As he lies dying, Jacob, or Israel as he is now called, gathers his twelve sons around him. He prophesies the establishment of the twelve tribes of Israel, telling each son which tribe he will lead and what the destiny of each tribe shall be.

While this passage, in which Jacob addresses his son, Judah, can be understood as a foretelling of the kingship of David, it is ultimately a messianic prophecy, words that would eventually be fulfilled with the coming of Christ. As Revelation 5:5 says of Jesus, he is the Lion of Judah, the Root of David.

Another Hebrew name for the lion, on the same order as "King of Beasts," is "Son of Pride." Today's gospel will relate the genealogy of Jesus Christ, showing his lineage—which has become our lineage—to be firmly rooted in Israel's rich history of salvation, while looking forward to the promise of his eternal messianic reign. He truly is the Son of Pride, our heritage and hope in which we rejoice.

Psalm 72:3-4,7-8,17

The psalmist extols the qualities of the messianic king.

This psalm probably was composed for a coronation or to celebrate the anniversary of a coronation. The hyperbole and great expectation expressed here certainly were not fulfilled in any kingship of Israel. Only in the Messiah could such hopes be realized.

Jesus Christ is this "Anointed One," the "Chosen of God" as no earthly ruler could ever be. He is the climax and fulfillment of all history. As such, his reign is to be eternal, and his rule over all "the tribes of the earth" (v. 17), not just the favored tribes of Israel.

The birth, passion, death, and resurrection of Jesus have ushered in this messianic age, and yet we watch and wait, especially in this time of heightened expectation, for our king to come in glory. It is in this wondrous advent that Christ will bring this mystery of salvation to completion.

Gospel — Matthew 1:1-17

The genealogy of Jesus, the Messiah of the line of David.

What is the purpose of reading the genealogy of Jesus? How can this help us prepare for his coming? One of the chief objectives of Matthew's Gospel is to show that Jesus is the Messiah of the line of David. Another of his goals is to show that this good news is not only for the Jews but for all peoples. Thus, Jesus' genealogy proves him to be both the son of David—and hence, the son of kings—and the son of Abraham—by whose descendants "all the nations of the earth shall find blessing" (Genesis 22:18).

This will for the salvation of humanity is shown to have existed through all time. Matthew cites three sets of fourteen generations each, giving witness to a God who has used human history to manifest his saving power. All generations are laid out before us, a sort of aerial view of history, in which we can now see God's plan of salvation. And even as God has been present throughout all time, so does he extend his loving sovereignty to people of all races and all nations. All are his family. We catch a passing glimpse, then, into the way our Creator has continually worked to draw all people and all things to himself.

Question: In what way could my knowledge of my own origins help me to grow spiritually?

Prayer: Lord, help me to trust in your power, your might, and your vision of time and eternity. Teach me and guide me, so that I might follow your path to salvation. Thank you, Lord. Amen.

Late Advent Weekday: December 18

Reading I — Jeremiah 23:5-8

From the house of David comes the salvation of Israel. "I will raise up a righteous shoot to David.... / This is the name they give him: / 'The LORD our justice.'"

The prophet Jeremiah lived during a period of Israel's history in which God's people were beset with great political upheaval and religious turmoil, due in part to the weak and corrupt leadership of some of the Judean kings. As a result, many of Jeremiah's prophecies look forward to a time when a good and just king shall once again sit on the throne. The ideal king, as Jeremiah describes him, is a righteous shoot sprouting from the line of David, righteous in the sense that he is at once legitimate and in conformity with the will of God. Jeremiah names this king "The LORD our justice" (23:6).

While Jeremiah's prophecies were originally meant to give the people of God hope during hard times, hope for the restoration of the glory of the Davidic kingship, there is deeper significance to these words. Justice, as used in this context, signifies more than mere equity. It connotes the very presence of God, his saving power at work in the midst of his people. Where there is justice, there, too, is the Lord. This king, then, is the Messiah, the Anointed One, the Just One of God's own choosing. This king truly is Emmanuel, God-with-us. Even as Jeremiah looked forward to a time when God would once again place on the throne of Israel a righteous king, a true son of David, so do we watch and wait for the coming of the king of righteousness, the Son of David himself.

Psalm 72:1,12-13,18-19

"Blessed be the Lord, the God of Israel, / who alone does wondrous deeds. / And blessed forever be his glorious name; / may the whole earth be filled with his glory. / Amen. Amen."

Though it might be translated as "so be it," amen can also mean "it is true" or "I confirm and agree with this statement." An amen used in the context of prayer, then, becomes a sort of confession of faith. Hence, the double amen that concludes this psalm becomes a solemn affirmation of all that has gone before.

We are told in this psalm that the God of Israel comes in justice to save his people. The psalmist's amen becomes our own joyous and grateful "Yes!" to that which we will soon celebrate, the mystery of salvation as it climaxes in the coming of the Messiah.

Gospel — Matthew 1:18-24

Mary conceives by the power of the Holy Spirit, and an angel tells Joseph that he need not fear taking Mary as his wife. Joseph names the child Jesus, because "he will save his people from their sins."

In today's gospel, the titles "son of God" and "son of David" are unified in the person of Jesus. Since he was conceived by the power of the Holy Spirit, Jesus is unmistakably the Son of God. At the same time, Joseph names the child, which, according to Jewish law, means that Joseph acknowledges Jesus to be his own son. Joseph is of the line of David, and so Jesus, too, becomes a son of David. Thus, Jesus is both Emmanuel and the promised Messiah of the house of David. He is the one who will "save his people from their sins" (2:21), fulfilling the covenant God had established with Moses.

Even as this passage treats of the "naming" of the Redeemer, it also enlarges upon the character of Joseph. Though he finds himself in the midst of tribulation and uncertainty, Joseph follows God's will and says "yes" to mystery. He may never be able to explain or understand what God is doing, but he trusts nonetheless. Spectacular results follow upon his show of faith: Old Testament prophecies are brought to fulfillment as Joseph's trust in God's word brings salvation to us all.

Question: Mother Teresa of Calcutta says that we should "give God permission" to use us as he will. Joseph gave God permission in saying yes to God's will. In what way can I "give God permission" to use me today?

Prayer: Help me to trust in you, Lord, that your will might become my own. I "give you permission" to use me as your instrument. Give me, in turn, the strength, courage and peace to do whatever it is you may ask. Thank you, Lord. Amen. Amen.

Late Advent Weekday: December 19

Reading I — Judges 13:2-7,24-25

Samson's mother conceives him through the power of God and consecrates him as a Nazirite. "It is he who will begin the deliverance of Israel."

Today's first reading is an annunciation story and, as such, has several parallels both in Hebrew Scripture and in the Gospel of Luke. The births of Ishmael (Genesis 16:7-16), Isaac (Genesis 18:1-15), John the Baptist (Luke 1:5-25), and Jesus (Luke 1:26-38) are heralded in similar fashion. In each instance, God works wonders in the most unlikely of circumstances, his will for salvation overcoming even the greatest of obstacles. The handmaid, the aged, the barren, and the virgin are all found to be with child. Each of these children shall play a part in the unfolding of salvation history, with the last of them, Jesus, bringing salvation to its fulfillment.

In the Advent liturgy, then, the figure of Samson foreshadows that of John the Baptist and, ultimately, Christ. In his miraculous conception, Samson is consecrated to God even from the womb, by virtue of the Nazirite vow that the Lord enjoins on his mother—that is, the injunction against strong drink, ritual impurity, and the use of a razor. Thus, Samson is destined to become a leader of his people in their struggles with the Philistines, and will take his place among the judges of Israel. These judges did not hand down rulings or pass sentences, but rather sought to restore righteousness to the people of God, to defend them against their enemies, and to give witness to the power and the will of God. While

Samson's strength bespeaks God's saving power, his sacrificial death defeated the enemy more thoroughly than he would have been able to in life. As he extends his arms to rock the pillars of the temple and bring destruction upon the Philistines, Samson foreshadows Jesus' passion and death on the cross, by which death would be destroyed forever.

Psalm 71:3-4,5-6,16-17

The psalmist pleads to be rescued from the wicked. "Fill me with your praise and I will sing your glory!"

Giving praise to God while one is under attack is difficult. Yet if we keep faith, adversity becomes a spiritual womb from which God can bring forth good. As we have seen throughout all of our history, from our youth even to now, God's loving care is with us despite all our hardships. Even as we trust God, he strengthens us and gives us peace.

We are called to have the courage of Samson, to trust in God, that he might break our chains of bitterness, despair, and anger. Even in the midst of our pain and imprisonment, we proclaim the victory that is ours. We always have before us the example of our Savior, who underwent suffering and death so that we all might know the glory of the Resurrection. We praise God for the triumph that is his, and which has become our own.

Gospel — Luke 1:5-25

Gabriel announces the birth and mission of John the Baptist.

Like Samson in today's first reading, John is set apart to serve God, by virtue of his designation as a Nazirite—"He will never drink wine or strong drink" (1:15). Through the power of the Holy Spirit, John speaks the word announcing the Word. "In the spirit and power of Elijah" (1:17), John heralds the end-time. It is his task "to turn the hearts of fathers to their children and the rebellious to the wisdom of the just, and to prepare a people well-disposed" (1:17). John sounds the call to repentance and rejoicing. God's advent is upon us, bringing us victory.

Question: John the Baptist calls us to a change of heart, to be renewed in preparation for Christ's coming. How have I heard and responded to this call during these weeks of Advent?

Prayer: Lord, give me a changed and renewed heart. Strengthen me in the face of all adversity and evil, and help me to rejoice in your victory. Thank you, Lord. Amen.

Late Advent Weekday: December 20

Reading I — Isaiah 7:10-14

Ahaz refuses to ask for a sign from God, while Isaiah prophesies the birth of the messiah.

In Isaiah's time, a sign was a revelation of God, giving special knowledge of God's power. It was a gift and reassurance that God was there, that God was speaking. It confirmed that people were on the right track and that they had been hearing God correctly and following God as they should.

When Ahaz refuses to follow Isaiah's lead and ask for a sign, he is refusing to trust in God's presence and gifts. Isaiah's forthright witness in faith to God's power stands out in contrast: he speaks out in prophecy that "the virgin shall be with child, and bear a son, and shall name him Immanuel" (7:14). Isaiah calls us to believe in a God who is with us, who answers our prayers, and who is using history to reveal himself to us. And Isaiah points to the virgin who will act in trust, giving birth to sign and sacrament, to mystery and to Church, as she follows God's will.

Psalm 24:1-2,3-4,5-6

God reveals himself to the one "whose hands are sinless, whose heart is clean, / who desires not what is vain."

This psalm is an example of what is known as a "gate," or entrance, liturgy. Its occasion is a procession into the Temple. In the course of a psalm of this type, a question is asked and a teaching given as to the qualities one must possess in order to come before the Lord. "Whose hands are sinless" (v. 4) signifies one who not only is innocent of wrongdoing but seeks to do justice as well. "Whose heart is clean" (v. 4) suggests one who possesses a purity of intention that extends to love and concern for one's neighbor. "Who desires not what is vain" (v. 4) indicates one who worships no one and nothing else but

God. Such a one is centered on God alone, seeking to know and love him intimately.

One of the titles given to Mary is "Gate of Heaven." She could also be known as the "entrance gate." She lived out this psalm, opening herself fully to receive and celebrate the Word of God. She was so centered on God and so loving that she nourished God with her own body, freely carrying out and carrying his will. She taught us what following God's law really does. She was one who acted in obedience, whose "Let it be done to me as you say" gave Jesus to us all.

Gospel — Luke 1:26-38

Gabriel announces to Mary that she is to be the mother of Jesus. Mary responds, "Let it be done to me as you say."

In today's gospel, we see that, through Mary's discipleship, the ultimate sign of God, Jesus Christ, is revealed. Mary's trust, obedience, and affirmative response to Gabriel's message are the catalysts through which the power of the Holy Spirit comes upon her. A new genesis, a new and unique creation, has come into being with the conception of Christ. The world is made anew with the one who will triumph over the fall of Adam and Eve.

Obedience to God's will is enormously powerful. It can open wide our being so that the king of glory might enter in and fill us more completely. It can open us to the power of the Holy Spirit to make of us a new and better creation. Mary's example gives us both joy and hope. We, too, can bear God more fully as we do his will.

Question: "Let it be done to me as you say." How would Mary's words apply to my own life?

Prayer: Lord, help me to follow Mary's example of love, trust and obedience, and so become a better disciple. Open wide my being, that I might be filled with your light and freed from the darkness of sin and death. Thank you, Lord. Amen.

Late Advent Weekday: December 21

Reading I — Song of Songs 2:8-14

The lover calls his beloved to celebrate new life.

While December 21 is traditionally the first day of winter, this reading plunges us into the midst of spring. Since the birth of Christ, our springtime has been eternal. The new creation and new life that Jesus has brought us continually freshens and revives a world rendered stark and bleak by the winter of sin and despair.

Now, our winter is past. The Lord calls us to arise, to come forth, to rejoice in the springtime of his love. He vaults across the mountains and leaps across the hills. His unbounded joy quickens us so that we, too, are renewed. We come to share in his spring, throwing open the doors and hastening forth to exult with him in eternity.

Alternate Reading — Zephaniah 3:14-18

Rejoice, Israel! Your Lord is in your midst, renewing you with his love.

It is the goal of every marriage that both husband and wife be continually renewed in their love. They seek to love in such a giving and caring manner that their capacity to love and find joy in each other is ever expanded and extended.

In this reading, the Lord's love for his people is expressed in such terms. His is a love which has liberated us from all that oppresses us, from all that would keep us from him because of fear and anxiety. His is a love so joyous that it gives us eternal happiness. His is a love so all-encompassing and urgent that he eagerly comes to dwell in our midst, to renew us by his presence and make us one with him forever.

Thus, God has brought us to perfect love. We celebrate with joy, for this truly is a marriage festival. God comes to us, renews us, and rejoices for love of us, all so that we might love and rejoice in him.

Psalm 33:2-3, 11-12, 20-21

"Cry out with joy in the Lord, you holy ones." God's loving care is eternal, and "in his holy name we trust."

God's holiness is what makes him so utterly unique. Such perfect holiness would separate God from our humanity, in that God is entirely "other" from us, his essence lying beyond us. Yet, in the coming of Jesus, we receive a special gift, a cause for great joy. It is a real human child that kicks and cries among the straw in the Bethlehem manger. God is God, and yet human as well. The "other" becomes one of "us," bringing to bear on our humanity the perfection of his divinity. This is the "plan of the Lord...the design of his heart" of which we sing in today's psalm. The void that would separate us from God is bridged, and we share in a holiness and a profound sense of joy that otherwise we never could have known.

Gospel — Luke 1:39-45

"When Elizabeth heard Mary's greeting, the baby stirred in her womb."

The word used to describe the movement that John makes can be understood as skipping or leaping, as if all nature, even the baby in the womb, dances for joy. As John the Baptist leaps with prophetic anticipation, Elizabeth cries out with joy. It is with unrestrained happiness that they greet the coming of the Lord. The time for rejoicing has come!

Question: "Joy to the world! The Lord has come." In today's readings, the words of this familiar carol become a reality. What can I do today to greet the Lord's coming with joy?

Prayer: Lord, help me to believe in your promises and to greet your glorious coming with joy. Give me, in the midst of my winter, your gift of springtime renewal, that I might ever grow in your love. Thank you, Lord. Amen.

Late Advent Weekday: December 22

Reading I — 1 Samuel 1:24-28

The Lord answers Hannah's prayer: she conceives and bears Samuel. "Now I, in turn, give him to the LORD."

The passage that immediately precedes today's reading relates the story of how the Lord answered Hannah's prayer, blessing her with the birth of a son (1 Samuel 1:1-20). Now, in gratitude, Hannah returns the gift the Lord has given her, dedicating her son Samuel for priestly service in the Temple. While her gifts of a bull, an ephah of flour, and a skin of wine would constitute an ample sacrifice of thanksgiving, there is nothing Hannah can do to thank God adequately for his favor, except to give entirely of herself and the blessing she has received.

In this season of rejoicing, we, too, come with Hannah to the altar. We have been given the saving Son of God. Yet what can we offer in return? What gift can we bring that would be adequate thanks for such a blessing? Christina Rossetti, in her poem *In the Bleak Midwinter,* supplies a simple, yet all-encompassing, answer: "What can I give him, / Poor as I am? / If I were a shepherd / I would bring a lamb, / If I were a Wise Man / I would do my part, / Yet what I can I give Him, / Give my heart."

Psalm — 1 Samuel 2:1, 4-5, 6-7, 8

Hannah, rejoicing that her prayers have been answered in the conception and birth of Samuel, praises God for his saving might: "My heart exults in the LORD, / my horn is exalted in my God."

This canticle bears great resemblance to Mary's own hymn of praise, the *Magnificat,* which will follow in today's gospel. Like Mary, Hannah is the Lord's handmaiden, lifted up from lowly estate by the power of God. She is one of the *anawim,* the poor and humble whose greatest joy is to do the will of God faithfully and to trust in him above all else.

Because of their faith and trust in God's saving power, Hannah and Mary were brought to victory. In Scripture, a horn is a symbol of strength. A raised or exalted horn indicates that God, in his great power, has lifted someone (in this case, Hannah) in triumph, to new esteem and dignity. Hannah's vindication in the birth of Samuel means that her line will continue for generations to come. Mary's triumph will mean that her line, and our line, will continue in the glory of eternal life. We have good cause to cry out in the words of today's response, "My heart rejoices in the Lord, my Savior!"

Gospel — Luke 1:46-56

In her canticle of thanksgiving, the Magnificat, *Mary glorifies God for his gift of salvation. "My being proclaims the greatness of the Lord."*

Just as knowledge of Hannah's situation adds to our appreciation of her hymn, so, too, our knowledge of Mary's role in God's plan for salvation helps us to appreciate the true depths of Mary's joy. Through Mary, God has saved the human race. Through Mary, God has fulfilled his covenant promises. Through Mary, God's kingdom has come. Indeed, God has worked great wonders through Mary, who rejoices to be the instrument and vessel of God's saving grace.

So it is that Mary strives to put into words the sheer depth and breadth of God's love. The Latin version of Mary's hymn, from which it derives its traditional title, begins, *"Magnificat anima mea Dominum..."* or "My soul magnifies the Lord...." Just as a magnifying glass enlarges objects viewed through its lens, Mary's rejoicing spirit becomes the lens through which we might behold the greatness of God and his infinite goodness. It is in and through Mary that we will see God become visibly, tangibly, and lovably human in the person of Jesus.

Question: What do Mary and Hannah teach me about discipleship?

Prayer: Lord God, you have visited your people with your saving power, giving us victory over sin and death through Jesus, your Son. Fill our hearts with praise of you, that we might always rejoice in your love. Thank you, Lord. Amen.

Late Advent Weekday: December 23

Reading I — Malachi 3:1-4,23-24

The messenger of the Lord is coming to purify and prepare all for the end of time, "For he is like the refiner's fire, / or like the fuller's lye."

A refiner's fire and a fuller's lye both serve the same purpose. In refining metal, fire's heat causes the impurities to rise to the top where they may be skimmed away. A fuller uses lye to wash the stains from cloth. Both the fire and the lye cleanse objects to render them fit for use. So are the people of God to be cleansed and purified, and the use to which they are to be put is to offer a sacrifice of praise.

Since worthy sacrifice to the Lord entails not only obedience to the law but sanctification and interior holiness as well, we, too, should be cleansed completely. What should we do, then, to become holy and worthy to sacrifice all that we do and all that we are to the coming Lord? The answer comes from John the Baptist himself: Reform your lives! Make straight the way of the Lord!

Psalm 25:4-5,8-9,10,14

"Your ways, O Lord, make known to me; / teach me your paths."

This psalm and its response demonstrate how, throughout time, God has answered his people's every need and every cry for help. The psalmist asks the Lord for guidance and wisdom, as it is the Lord who shows the way. He thanks the Lord for his faithfulness to those who keep his covenant. To each of these thoughts, the response is, "Lift up your heads and see; / your redemption is near at hand."

Redemption has been God's answer to his people throughout all of salvation history. Even when we cannot comprehend God's plan or fail to understand how the circumstances of our life can possibly be a part of it, we see before us the compassionate Lord who suffered and died for us. We know that, even now, he suffers when we suffer. He invites us to hand our burdens over to him and to lift up our heads to behold him, risen and triumphant, standing at our side with his saving strength.

Gospel — Luke 1:57-66

Great wonders surround the birth and naming of John the Baptist. "All who heard stored these things in their hearts, saying, 'What will this child be?'"

We see in this reading the great signs which herald the coming of God's chosen ones. Elizabeth, childless up until now, has conceived in spite of her advanced years and given birth to a son. Both Elizabeth and Zechariah choose to call the child John—meaning "Yahweh has given grace"—rather than name the boy after his father or some other male relative or ancestor. Zechariah, who for months had been mute, suddenly speaks again, giving praise to God. Wonder upon wonder produce an atmosphere of anticipatory awe. Obviously, God has intervened here, touching human history. What can all this mean? Why is this child so important?

We can answer these questions. We know "what this child will be" and that the wonders revealed here will be as nothing compared to those yet to come. Awe and amazement are as much a part of the spirituality of Advent as is joyous anticipation. We are called in this season to gaze in wonderment at the mystery that has been revealed to us, a mystery that continues to unfold in our midst: God has given us the supreme grace of the healing Word, God's own presence, come to dwell among us.

Question: The communion antiphon for today's liturgy is: "I stand at the door and knock, says the Lord. If anyone hears my voice and opens the door, I will come in and sit down to supper with him and he with me" (Revelation 3:20). In light of today's readings, how would I apply this verse to myself?

Prayer: God of signs and wonders, you have shown yourself and spoken to your people throughout the ages. Even as you once came to dwell among us, so will you return to fulfill all that you have promised. Fill us with awe at the mystery of your incarnation, and help us to live in joyful anticipation of the glory yet to be revealed. Thank you, Lord. Amen.

Late Advent Weekday: December 24

Reading I — 2 Samuel 7:1-5,8-11,16

David is told that he should not build a house for the Lord, for the Lord will make of David a "house," a messianic dynasty.

While the birth of Jesus is a crowning event in salvation history, God's preparations for the coming of his son go back to the beginning of time. One of the most important of these preparations was God's covenant relationship with his chosen people. As it is understood in Hebrew Scripture, a covenant is a ritual contract in which two parties enter into a relationship and agree to fulfill certain obligations to each other. God "contracted" with the Jews to be their God, to help and save them, and they, in turn, would be his people and follow his law.

Israel's covenant with God had deep ramifications. The covenant bond represented, in effect, a blood relationship between God and his people. They were his kinsmen, members of his family. Hence, they were to have an intimate love for God like that of a husband for his wife, or a mother for her child. It was to be as if, as the prophet Jeremiah said, the law of God were written on the hearts of his people, not merely inscribed on the stone tablets kept in the Ark. God's people themselves were to be the Ark of the Covenant.

So it is that even as David dreams of building a splendid new house in which the Ark of the Covenant might reside, God makes it known that he has another dwelling place in mind. Whereas earthly houses will crumble in time, God promises to establish David and his house as his dwelling for all eternity. God will abide with David, and in time, this family line will bring to bear God himself in the Word made flesh. Thus it is that God will inscribe not only his law, but his very divinity, on the hearts of his people, transforming them and making them one with himself.

Psalm 89:2-3,4-5,27,29

God has made an eternal covenant with his people: "For you have said, 'My kindness is established forever.'"

In establishing a covenant with his people, God promised that his saving power would be with them. Hence, salvation is always a gift of God. It isn't conditional upon our actions, but rather is freely given by God. The establishment of an eternal covenant between God and humanity has been realized in the person of Jesus Christ, making all people members of God's family. In the Old Covenant, the blood of sacrifice linked us with God. Now, in the New Covenant, Jesus has offered his blood to form the bond of union between us and God, a covenant that endures forever. God has fulfilled the promise he made to save and redeem us. We are his beloved children. God's covenant with us in Christ is the most unconditional and loving gift we will ever receive.

Gospel — Luke 1:67-79

Zechariah blesses the God who has kept his covenant with his people. "He, the Dayspring, shall visit us in his mercy / To shine on those who sit in darkness and in the shadow of death, / to guide our feet into the way of peace."

This final reading summarizes some of the more important messages of Advent. Zechariah is speaking in prophecy, that is, he is speaking God's word, speaking on behalf of the Lord with a message for God's people. This message is important, for it has the basic attribute of prophecy: it comes from God to build up the Church.

This is God's word: God has come as he promised throughout the ages, bringing salvation to bear on all people. The incredible mercy of God has rescued us so that we are free to worship him. Zechariah's son, John the Baptist, is to prepare God's way, telling of this salvation through the forgiveness of sin. As salvation bears fruit in our own lives, we will grow in the completeness of peace.

This is the word, the Word that has come, that has advented into our midst. We have been, we are being, and we will be built up by this message—that is, if we accept it. Accepting it means living Advent, living out this Advent message. We say "yes" to salvation. We say "no" to perdition, to loss of holiness, to sin. We proclaim the Lord. And as we do so, again the light breaks, again the darkness is shattered, again the Daystar bursts, shines, and pours forth over our many Bethlehems. Christ is born.

Question: What has the message of this Advent been for me, and how will I act on this message?

Prayer: Thank you, Lord, for this season of Advent. Fill me with your Holy Spirit, that I might become all that you would want me to be. Bring me to rebirth and renewal in the glory of your love, and let me show forth your light, shining in the darkness as a sign of your covenant. Grant me the gift of your peace this Christmas Eve, that I may truly rest with you. *Maranatha*, come Lord Jesus! Amen.